# ABOVE SAN FRANCISCO

By Robert Cameron

A new collection of nostalgic and contemporary
aerial photographs of the Bay Area

Cameron and Company, San Francisco, California

Such a book as this does not reach publication without more than the usual amount of cooperation
from many people. So, for their encouragement and expertise I thank the following:

Hatsuro Aizawa, Robert Burger, Lex Byers, William D. Ganslen, John Goy, Gladys Hansen, Bill Stroh,
Willi Maier, Michael Murphy, Douglas Pirie, Jerry Rumburg, Carol Thares, Leonard Zuras
and especially pilots:
Pete Breinig, Dan Dugan, Steve Egger, Dave Ferguson, Ken Hughes,
Bill Knott, Bob McKeegan, Frank Shafer, Steve Sullivan
Balloonist: Brent Stockwell

CAMERON AND COMPANY
235 Montgomery Street
San Francisco, California 94104

Library of Congress Catalog Number: 70-103848
Above San Francisco ISBN 0-918684-05-6
©1980 by Robert W. Cameron and Company, Inc. All rights reserved.

First Printing, 1975
Second Printing, 1976
Third Printing, 1977
Fourth Printing, 1978
Fifth Printing, 1978
Sixth Printing, 1979
Seventh Printing, 1980
Eighth Printing, 1981
Ninth Printing, 1981
Tenth Printing, 1982
Eleventh Printing, 1983

Book design by Jane Olaug Kristiansen

Color Processing by Cady Color Lab & Faulkner Color Lab
Typography by ReederType, Inc., Fremont, California
Color Separation and Printing by Dai Nippon Printing Co., Tokyo, Japan

TABLE OF CONTENTS

# AMERICA: THE GODLIKE VIEW

## By Alistair Cooke

Nobody, not even Robert Cameron, asked me to write this foreword.

I am doing it because, in the first volume of ABOVE SAN FRANCISCO, he attempted something quite unique in the history of photography, and in this second volume he has achieved it, and gone beyond it.

It seems to me that he has done nothing less than what Leonardo had hoped to do with his attempts to invent a flying machine: which, according to his notebooks, was not simply to enjoy the sensuous pleasures of flight but to see the earth in relation to its man-made compounds as the eagles saw it.

Of course, people have always had an itch to get above the trees and see the wood. Hence the telescope on the Empire State Building, the Top O' The . . . . cocktail bars, the innumerable "Inspiration Points" in every National Park and Forest, and on every little mountain overlooking a batch of second-growth pine and a picnic ground. San Francisco, on account of its swooping hills and the sudden vistas they provide, must be the tourist's All-American inspiration point, judging from the mounds of discarded film packages lying everywhere between the Peninsula reservoir, the crest of Lombard Street and the Golden Gate Bridge.

Cameron is, so far as I know, the first person to exploit helicopter photography as a means of combining the large, but myopic, view of the map-maker and the geographer with the intimate view of a man on his rooftop. No other city on earth has been so thoroughly—never mind lovingly—observed from the air as Cameron observed it in his first volume.

This second volume, I believe, is a more considerable achievment still. When I heard that Cameron was going to do it, I assumed that his insatiable affection for such local treasures as the Delta, Nob Hill and Daly City (not to mention his balloon fetish) had got the better of him. More of the same.

Not so. This book is a photographic landmark, in that it substitutes, for the city planner's glib sketches of what a building or a park or a town MIGHT look like, a relentless record of what it DOES look like after Twentieth Century man has had his fling with one peninsula and its surrounding littoral.

In this second volume, Cameron has introduced two photographic novelties that greatly clarify the history of what we now call "urban development." First, he has had the wit to set the remarkable panoramas of Eadweard Muybridge against his own pictures, taken nearly a century later, from the same vantage points. There is revealing stuff here that ought to be on the desk of every architect and ecologist in the country.

Secondly, he has given a new dimension to both the Cameron and Muybridge views of a growing city by letting us see it as it looks not to the humble eagle but to the astronaut; by reprinting, that is, the high-altitude photographs of the National Aeronautics and Space Administration and its Skylab 4, which keeps a godlike watch on the earth from 260 miles up.

Muybridge (1830-1904) is very much worth a passing tribute. He was one of those obscure English eccentrics who parlayed a dotty hobby and a Victorian ferocity for hard work into lasting fame. He emigrated in his youth and set up an antiquarian book business in San Francisco. He was nearly killed in a stagecoach accident and went back to England to be treated. His doctor, possessing none of the clinical or pharmacological expertise of our time, blithely recommended a total cure in the form of "fresh" air and sensible sweat. So Muybridge junked the book business and set himself up as a scenic photographer, teaching himself the while a great deal about chemical formulae and camera techniques. By now, his reputation as a pioneer photographer is secure, first for his panoramas of Yosemite but most of all for the immortal series of pictures that won for Leland Stanford a whacking bet of $25,000 by proving that a horse in full stride has all its four feet off the ground. A first edition of Muybridge's ANIMAL LOCOMOTION is only a little less precious today than the first edition of Boswell's Johnson.

The NASA pictures are of two kinds. The U-2 photographs were taken from a plane at 65,000 feet, and their fine definition is due to the excellence of the equipment and to new techniques in fast-flying exposure. As for the Skylab 4 pictures, we might be forgiven for guessing that what they might gain in scale they would lose in precision. Their definition is, in fact, uncanny, as anyone can see who places a strong lens over any square inch of the pictures and is alarmed to recognize his own house. This microscopic definition is due to incomparable lenses and to a total absence of camera motion, since the camera platform is beyond the gravisphere and hangs motionless in space.

Cameron himself may be surprised to hear that the impulse that sent him off to Muybridge and NASA is what gives this new volume its novelty and its importance. This does not matter too much. An artist responding to his best (as also his worst) impulses is usually unconscious of the raw material that drives and engrosses him.

In any case, he has produced here a thing of beauty and a first-rate sociological document. If he often dwells, as he did in the first volume, on favorite panoramas of great splendor or tenderness, he also charts relentlessly the godawful mess that builders and "developers" have made of large stretches of a lovely landscape. He has given us a rousing celebration of what Frank Lloyd Wright saw as the true aim of architecture: "to design buildings that follow, or seem to grow out of, the essential character of the terrain they inhabit." And he has also put down a record of what the Industrial Revolution, in its expensive Twentieth Century aftermath, has done to one famous part of the livable earth.

It is both a joy and a warning.

This remarkable photograph (actually a mosaic of several photographs) was made from the famous N.A.S.A. U-2 observation plane from a height of 65,000 feet. Its extraordinary clarity is due to haze-cutting infra-red film, which, however, makes green appear red.

# SAN FRANCISCO

This evening aspect of the City reveals it in the forty-five minutes or so known to photographers as "golden light." Some of the Presidio's residences are seen in the foreground.

Eadweard Muybridge made the panoramic photographs on Pages 12, 14, 16, 18, 20, and 22 from the roof of the Mark Hopkins residence on Nob Hill in January of 1877. This view shows the northwest corner of California and Mason Streets, where James Flood was beginning to build his house. Up California Street are the Huntington and Crocker houses, and the interesting "spite fence" can be seen between them. Charles Crocker, who wanted to own all the land on his block, built the 40-foot enclosure around the house of Nicholas Yung, who refused to sell. Yung lived in the house until his death three years later.

From roughly the same vantage point used by Muybridge (the Mark Hopkins residence having been replaced by the Hotel Mark Hopkins), is California Street today. The James Flood mansion was gutted but rebuilt after the 1906 Fire and is today the Pacific Union Club. Huntington Park replaced Huntington's home, which was also destroyed in 1906, as was the Crocker home. Grace Cathedral stands on the property given by the Crocker family to Episcopal Diocese.

Looking north down the valley between Telegraph and Russian Hills, Mason Street
leads to Fisherman's Wharf and beyond, in the Bay, Alcatraz and Angel Islands.

Past the roof of the Fairmont Hotel one cannot help but get a "built-up"
feeling as we see the sky-scraping apartment buildings on Russian Hill.

As the Cable Car tracks lead down California Street, they pass Old St. Mary's, one of the few remaining and recognizable structures in these pictures. The Montgomery Block, famous for housing many artists and writers, was a survivor of the 1906 Fire and can be seen looking east toward Yerba Buena Island. It was torn down in the 1950's and the Transamerica Pyramid now stands on its location. Three-masters from all over the world are moored at the Embarcadero.

On the corner of Powell and California Streets stands the red brick University Club, across from the Fairmont Hotel Gardens. Further down California is Old St. Mary's peeking around the Hartford Building. To the left of the Transamerica Pyramid in the Bay is Treasure Island, built for the 1939 World's Fair and now occupied by the Navy. Some of the other buildings in the upper right quadrant are the Holiday Inn Hotel, the Alcoa Building, and the International Building.

The roof in the immediate foreground is that of the Leland Stanford residence. Further out toward the Bay is the Selby Shot Tower, in which lead bullets were made as they fell in molten form to the ground. Jack London was born nearby at Third and Brannan in 1876. The large building is the Palace Hotel, built by William Ralston in 1875 — it was gutted in the 1906 Fire but rebuilt, and stands today at Market and New Montgomery Streets.

A bit of the new and elegant Stanford Court Hotel can be seen here. Past it the skyline is dominated by many skyscrapers, tallest of which are the Bank of America Building, the Wells Fargo Building, and Crocker Tower. To the right are the Hyatt Union Square Hotel and the 450 Sutter Building, which is almost wholly occupied by doctors and dentists.

As Powell Street descends steeply toward Market it passes Union Square and ends at "Lucky" Baldwin's Theatre-Hotel, which was destroyed by fire in 1898. To the right on Post at Mason is the Congregational Church, and it still stands today, but without its steeple, which was toppled by the earthquake.

Past the Grosvenor House Apartments, more sky-piercing hotels—from left to right: the Holiday Inn, the Sir Francis Drake, the St. Francis, and the Hilton Tower. To the right rear is the Fox Plaza at Larkin and Market Streets.

Pine Street dominates this photograph as it rolls westward past many lavish and elegant homes, in which, only thirty years after settling of the city, San Franciscans began to live a secure and easy life.

Toward Twin Peaks we see the large dark Federal Building and to its right the new Sutro Tower. The white structure, center, is New St. Mary's Cathedral, and to its right on the skyline are U.C. Hospital and Lone Mountain College.

RUINS OF SAN FRANCISCO
NOB HILL IN FOREGROUND
FROM LAWRENCE CAPTIVE AIRSHIP
1500 FEET ELEVATION
MAY 29, 1906.

COPYRIGHT 1906
GEO. R. LAWRENCE CO.
CHICAGO.

NEW YORK    WASHINGTON    SAN FRANCISCO

COPYRIGHTED 1909 BY
E. J. WATERS AERIAL PHOTOGRAPH Co
OPERATING UNDER GEO. R. LAWRENCE PATENT.

24

San Francisco pictured from a Captive Balloon one month and eleven days after the Earthquake-Fire of 1906. This view is the best known record of the devastation of the City.

The resiliency of San Francisco is demonstrated by another Captive Balloon picture of the City "rising from its ashes." And in only three years.

SAN FRANCISCO—APRIL 1906
THREE YEARS AFTER
1000 FEET ABOVE JONES & WASHINGTON STS.

The original caption for this picture was: "Aeroplane view main group of exhibit palaces, Panama-Pacific International Exposition, from Silas Christofferson's aeroplane, at an altitude of 1500 feet." It should be added that the photograph was taken in 1914 by Gabriel Moulin and subsequently hand-colored.

City Hall, center, is surrounded by Fox Plaza and Civic Auditorium at left, the Opera House and the Veteran's Building behind it, the public library and the old Federal Building in the foreground. Brooks Hall Convention Center is under the green area.

Famous stores surround Union Square. The new St. Francis Tower is at left, the Sir Francis Drake, Holiday Inn, and Hyatt hotels are to the right. A municipal parking area lies beneath the square.

Embarcadero Center's Golden Gateway and Tennis Club looks toward the new Hyatt Regency Hotel. To the right of center in background is One Embarcadero Center, sometimes referred to as Rockefeller Center West.

Street merchants draw a Sunday crowd to Justin Herman Plaza at the foot of Market Street. The Vaillancourt Fountain appears past the top of the Ferry Building tower.

Hyde Street Pier at Fisherman's Wharf is a State Historical Park. Tied up there for tourists are the lumber schooner Thayer, the steam schooner Wapama and ferryboat Eureka.

Fort Mason (foreground) got its name in 1847. An Army debarkation point for W.W. II and the Korean War, it is now headquarters of the Golden Gate National Recreation Area. The Maritime Museum looks out over Aquatic Park—back of it is Ghirardelli Square. To the left is the Cannery, Fisherman's Wharf and the Hyde Street Pier. The strange-looking building at the end of the pier (lower left) housed criminals while they waited for the boat to transfer them to Alcatraz Federal Prison, which opened in 1934 and closed in 1963.

Small foreign cars by the hundreds decorate an otherwise empty pier, which seems to have been bumped by something large.

The dynamism of financial district buildings seems exaggerated from the air. Commuters pour through the East Bay Terminal in foreground.

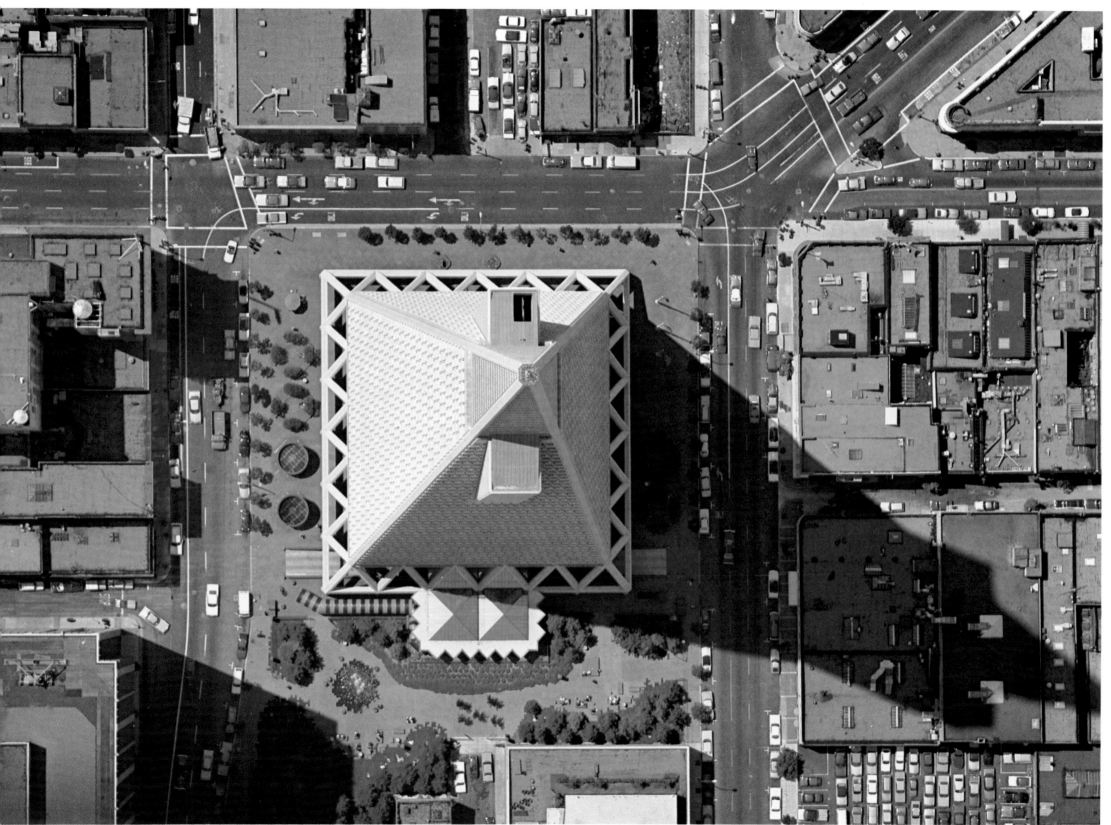

The proud Pyramid is squashed by a long-focus lens.

Just before the City's lights come on, the sun's last rays create a theatrical backdrop.

38

Two aerial studies of Telegraph Hill and Coit Tower, now a tourist haven but once the vantage point from which arriving vessels were first seen as they came through the Gate. Signals were raced to the marts of Montgomery Street from here.

A new Southern Pacific Station replaces the handsome old one at rear. An unfinished freeway is always an arresting sight, this one resembles a severed snake as it curves around China Basin.

The Yerba Buena Center has been renamed the George Moscone Convention Center. Built to meet the increasing need for convention and exhibit space, it is largely underground. Structure in the foreground is the San Francisco Racquet Club.

41

Russian Hill looks out over practically everything. The large flat
red building in the foreground is the
Cable Car Barn and Museum.

The Spreckels Mansion at right faces Lafayette Park. Behind it, Pacific Heights drops down toward the Marina and the Bay.

Most of the homes in this Pacific Heights location have some kind of view of the Bay even if it has to be seen out of a bay window.

Center-of-the-block greenery typifies Cow Hollow neighborhoods.

Bush Street at center is the "one-way" access for commuters to the financial district as they drive to it in the morning. It is flanked by Pine on the left and Sutter on the right, which are "one-way" streets coming back in the evening. Perpendicular to them at bottom of the picture is Larkin Street.

The traditional Cherry Blossom Festival Parade passes by Japan Town on Post Street. Busy Geary Street on right hums its way up Cathedral Hill.

At the center is the University of San Francisco and across Turk Boulevard is Lone Mountain College. In the distance the wooded Presidio lies at the edge of the Bay.

Looking past the De Young Museum and the Music Concourse are African Hall, Morrison Planetarium, Steinhart Aquarium, and California Academy of Sciences. At the base of Mt. Sutro in background is the University of California Medical Center.

Sutro Tower, a 977 foot structure atop Mt. Sutro, was completed in 1973. It
beams the signals of four FM radio stations and seven television stations.

This unusual aspect of the residential area around Twin Peaks looking northwest has Mt. Davidson at left and Mt. Sutro at right.

As Route 101 traffic speeds down to the Peninsula, it bends around
Potrero Hill, famous for enjoying the sunniest weather in the City.

Having just left the Daly City terminal, this Bay Area Rapid Transit train enters a tunnel that takes it under the Bay and through the hills to Concord, some 36 miles away. B.A.R.T. services over 165,000 commuters daily.

Polk Street looking north toward the Bay.

Union Street looking east toward the Bay.

What can be said about streets? Some are famous for shopping, some for eating, some for business and some for just strolling. On the next five pages are streets of all kinds. They are too diverse to be described in detail so they will be identified.

This photograph asks only that you draw your own conclusions.

Five golf courses surround Lake Merced at the San Mateo county line; they are, starting in foreground and clock-wise: Lake Merced Golf and Country Club, Olympic Country Club (Ocean Course and Lakeside Course), Harding Park Municipal Golf Course, and the San Francisco Golf Club.

This rocky beach near Lands End is a favorite of health addicts on sunny days.

The blimp during its periodic visits is based at Oakland Airport; here it has crossed the Bay to visit the San Francisco Financial District.

Fleecy forerunners of the summer fog partially obscure the sunlit city from 5,000 feet

# SAN FRANCISCO BAY

This close-up of the Golden Gate Bridge south tower shows *Traveler*, a mechanism for replacing vertical cables. It takes four years to replace them all.

On her maiden voyage, the cruise liner Pacific Princess enters the Golden Gate for the first time and is greeted by the blimp.

The Aircraft Carrier Coral Sea, "San Francisco's Own" returns after eight months in the South Pacific, where she helped evacuate South Viet Nam. Look closely to see a yellow ribbon on Coit Tower, put there by the wives and sweethearts of the crewmen.

Vacant Alcatraz on some days receives as many as 2,400 visitors. A group seen here among the flowers is escorted by National Park Rangers. At left, an evening shot of the problem island.

Golden Hinde II, a replica of the vessel Sir Francis Drake sailed past the fog-bound Golden Gate in 1579. Christened by Prince Philip in England in 1973, she sailed through the Panama Canal to San Francisco where she was greeted by practically every boat in the Bay.

On opening day of the yachting season, hospitable Hospital Cove at Angel Island greets all who wish to moor here to "the largest floating cocktail party anywhere."

A happy family of sea lions look curiously at the helicopter from Seal Rock off Land's End and the Cliff House. The rocks are white with guano and it is said that Alcatraz looked like this when it was first discovered.

In 1939, the Golden Gate International Exposition opened on man-made Treasure Island, which connects to Yerba Buena Island. Plans to build an airport on it fell through, and it is now occupied by the Navy.

Due west of the Golden Gate lie the Farallone Islands, certainly the loneliest bit of real estate in San Francisco County. The Coast Guard maintains a lighthouse, and the Navy has a radar installation here. They are federal property and a National Fish and Game Preserve.

# HIGH ABOVE SAN FRANCISCO

Flowing golden light changes the character of a familiar scene from 10,000 feet.
The sun glances off windshields as the traffic enters Marin County below.

The Easter Saturday balloon race takes place at Morgan Hill. Here in the next four pages are the contestants in various stages of inflation and flight.

Up, up and away!

A daredevil hanglider prepares to cut loose from his host.

The shadows are long because it's 7:00 in the morning, and that's when the wind can be dependably under 10 miles per hour, the balloonist's limit.

A balloon match race across the bay was aborted for lack of wind and landed this contestant on the Marina Green.

A lonely little island named Red Rock is just south of Richmond-San Rafael Bridge. Fog obscures all but the top of Mount Tamalpais.

This U-2 shot has the afternoon fog entering the Golden Gate, taken from 65,000 feet on infra-red film. Across is the East Bay and Peninsula.

Aerial photography at its ultimate refinement. From Skylab 4,270 miles up in space, this composite includes both Santa Rosa and Tracy. Notice the mothball fleet in the Sacramento River Delta.

This oblique shot departs from the norm of the usual U-2 exposure. Of particular interest is the Sierra Nevada at the top, and beyond that the black area demonstrates the curvature of the earth.

# SOUTH BAY

Atop Mt. Hamilton, the University of California's Lick Observatory houses the second largest refracting telescope in the world. Founded by James Lick it was completed in 1888; he lies buried here.

Patterns of houses near the beach stretch off toward the Peninsula. The two traffic arteries are Skyline Boulevard to the right and Highway 280 to the left.

South San Francisco was incorporated to be an industrial city. Originally a stage coach stop, it controlled a toll road to San Francisco. The handsome City Hall at center is a western variation on Philadelphia's Independence Hall.

The ever-expanding San Francisco International Airport handles 24,000,000 passengers every year.

Filoli is the magnificent 1,714 acre estate deeded by Lurline Matson Roth in 1975 to the National Trust for Historic Preservation. Beyond to the north are the reservoirs that furnish San Francisco with its water.

Looking over beautiful residences in the San Carlos Hills is the San Francisco skyline.

Halfway down the Peninsula is Marine World, with lions and tigers as well as dolphins and whales.

The structure in foreground houses Howard Hughes' secret barge, built to help raise the
Russian atomic submarine sunk in the Pacific. In background is a storage pile of salt.

El Camino Real runs south past Menlo Park in the foreground.
Palo Alto is at the left rear, and Stanford University campus is at the right.

Radar installation reads signals from Skylabs. Past it in the distance is Stanford University.

Super highways snake through Los Gatos southwest of San Jose. La Rinconada Golf Club is at the top left and the large body of water to the right is Vasona Reservoir.

In the East San Jose Foothills is Mount Saint Joseph Carmelite Seminary.

Over 500,000 attend the Santa Clara County Fair, high point of which is the "Demolition Derby."

N.A.S.A.-Ames Research Center at Moffett Field is also occupied by the Navy. Structure in the foreground is the largest wind tunnel in the free world. It was used in testing the Space Shuttle, a plane for commuting in space. The large hangar at rear was built for the dirigible Macon, which swamped and went down in Big Sur in 1935. It has housed many dirigibles since, and is so big that under certain conditions it rains inside of it.

Visitors are attracted to the Winchester Mystery House in San Jose. It has been added onto over the years, it now has 1,000 rooms.

An airliner makes its approach to the San Jose Airport, seen in the distance. Work in progress on the interchange below typifies this burgeoning community.

Looking east toward the San Jose airport, sections of Sunnyvale and Santa Clara are seen in left and right foreground.

San Jose State University with enrollment of 25,000 was originally chartered as Minns' Evening Normal School in 1857. It has changed names six times since then.

Novitiate Winery and Vineyard in Los Gatos is high above Lexington Reservoir.

Paul Masson Vineyards in Saratoga, founded in 1852, has over 4,500 acres under vines.

ALAMEDA-CONTRA COSTA

Mount Diablo sports a temporary mantle of snow. In the distance is the Sacramento River Delta.

Lake Merritt dominates the landscape of downtown Oakland.

At lower right is Oakland Auditorium, next to it with much green area
is the Oakland Museum. Across the street is the Alameda County Court House.

Near downtown Oakland this housing development is an example of urban renewal.

Below right is the Oakland Paramount; completely restored, it is now the handsomest large theatre in the Bay Area. Kaiser Center at Upper left.

Two B.A.R.T. trains pass each other at Oakland West station, first stop east of the Bay tunnel.

Porto Bello homes and marina on the Oakland Estuary. Flag at left is on Tribune Tower.

On the Oakland Estuary a Seatrain ocean freighter is simultaneously loaded and unloaded of containers for shipment to or from the East Coast by rail.

In foreground is the fast-changing Jack London Square area. Across the Oakland Estuary is Alameda.

The Aircraft Carrier Enterprise lies below at Alameda Naval Air Station. Alongside of it is the Aircraft Carrier Ranger.

Walnut Creek, formerly a commuter's bedroom community, is now a bustling city.

The Benecia-Martinez Bridge spans Carquinez Strait. Across the strait is Solano County.

Carquinez Bridge connects Crockett in foreground and Vallejo. Mare Island Naval Shipyard is at upper left.

Bayside homes at Point Richmond look southwest toward the Golden Gate.

Standard Oil's tank farm and refinery command a view of the East Bay shoreline.

Mothball fleet of World War II ships rides at anchor in Suisun Bay. From the one-time high of 500 ships, numbers have now dropped to around 100.

Benicia, first capital of California, is now a large foreign automobile storage terminal.

North of Concord looking toward the Sacramento River Delta. Port Chicago is in the distance at right.

Concord Pavilion presents entertainment of all kinds. Green section of ampitheatre is seating fashioned of sod.

Route 24 and B.A.R.T. station at Lafayette.

Past Orinda center and B.A.R.T. station are the San Pablo and Briones Reservoirs.

Near Alamo on Route 680 is Rossmoor Leisure World retirement community.

High in the hills is Lafayette Reservoir Recreation Area.

NAPA - MARIN - SONOMA

Sun-tipped clouds almost obscure Sausalito and Richardson Bay Bridge.

Looking south to San Francisco over Richardson Bay is Belvedere on left and Sausalito on right.

Belle Marin Keys near Marin County Center. Look west to Mount Tamalpais.

In foreground, preparations are made for the Marin County Fair at County Center which was designed by Frank Lloyd Wright. Highway 101 leads south to San Francisco.

144

The San Rafael Channel goes up to San Rafael, oldest city in Marin County.

Century-old Bolinas just north of Stinson Beach was once a lumber center; it is now a quaint and quiet village. The Bolinas Lagoon is a Bird Sanctuary.

This high view is of Sonoma as Valley of the Moon stretches southward.

Looking South from Mt. Tamalpais past Richardson Bay toward the City after a rare snowfall.

On the Marin side of San Pablo Strait are a gravel quarry and McNears Beach. In the distance the Peacock Gap Golf and Country Club.

Sear's Point Raceway near Sonoma is 2 ½ miles long on 700 acres. The best High Performance Race Driving School in the country is located here.

Located near the little town of Glen Ellen in the Sonoma Valley is the Jack London Ranch now a State Park. 275,000 visitors come here every year.

The walls of burned-out Wolf House built by Jack London still stand. It is said that arsonists were responsible for the fire.

Silverado, site of San Francisco Bay Area's only Tour-Pro Golf Tournament—the Anheuser-Busch Golf Classic.

Inglenook Winery in Rutherford is a vine-covered building built in 1879 by Gustave Niebaum.

The Napa Valley's Christian Brothers Winery and aging cellars were built over a century ago. It houses antique winery equipment and Brother Timothy's corkscrew collection.

Robert Mondavi Winery's first crush was in 1966. Located in Oakville, it boasts an art gallery and facilities for musical events.

Berenger's Winery in St. Helena boasts a 17 room manor house for tourists' tasting. It was operated by four generations of the family for over a hundred years. Further up Main Street is Christian Brothers' Greystone Cellars.

Sterling Vineyards Winery is Modern Mediterranean architecturally. Perched on a hill above Calistoga it is reached by tramway.